DATE DUE

MAR 1 9 2003			

DEMCO 38-297

GUYS' GUIDES

Dating and Relating

A Guy's Guide to Girls

Tara E. Kelly

the rosen publishing group's
rosen central
new york

Thanks to my parents—for dating and relating successfully—and to my editor, Erin Hovanec at Rosen Publishing, for guiding me through this guide.

Published in 2000 by The Rosen Publishing Group, Inc.
29 East 21st Street, New York, NY 10010

Library of Congress Cataloging-in-Publication Data

Kelly, Tara E.
        Dating and relating : a guy's guide to girls / Tara E. Kelly.
              p. cm. — (Guys' guides)
        Includes bibliographical references and index.
    Summary: Discusses boys' relationships to girls as they begin adolescence, including puberty, friendships, dating, and sex.
        ISBN 0-8239-3110-2 (lib. bdg.)
      1. Dating (Social customs)—Juvenile literature. 2. Interpersonal relations in adolescence—Juvenile literature. 3. Puberty—Juvenile literature. 4. Teenage boys—Conduct of life—Juvenile literature. [1. Dating (Social customs) 2. Interpersonal relations. 3. Puberty. 4. Conduct of life.] I. Title. II. Series.

HQ801 .K453 1999
646.7'7 21—dc21
                                                                    99-042088

Manufactured in the United States of America

Contents

>> About This Book <<

It's not easy being a guy these days. You're expected to be buff, studly, and masculine, but at the same time, you're supposed to be sensitive, thoughtful, and un-macho. And that's not all. You have to juggle all of this while you're wading through the shark-infested waters of middle school. So not only are you dealing with raging hormones, cliques and geeks, and body changes, but you're also supposed to figure out how to be a Good Guy. As if anyone is even sure what that means anyway. It's enough to make you wish for the caveman days, when guys just grunted and wrestled mammoths with their bare hands and stuff.

Being an adolescent is complicated. Take girls, for example. Just five minutes ago—or so it seems—they weren't much different from you and your buddies. Now, suddenly you can't keep your eyes off them, and other parts of your body have taken an interest too. Or maybe you're not interested in girls yet, and you're worried about when you will be. Then there's figuring out where you fit into the middle school world. Are you a jock, a brain, or what? And how come it seems that someone else gets to decide for you? What's up with that?

Yeah, it's tough. Still, you're a smart guy, and you'll figure it all out. That's not to say that we can't all use a hand. That's where this book comes in. It's sort of a cheat sheet for all the big tests that your middle school years throw at you. Use it to help you get through the amazing maze of your life—and to come out alive on the other side.

If you are reading this book, it is probably because you have started to realize that girls might not be so bad after all. If you are reading this book, you probably know that girls aren't made of sugar and spice and everything nice. If you are reading this book, it is probably because you sense that the whole girl thing is way more complicated than you ever imagined.

But fear not! Help is here in the form of a real live girl. By the time I'm done with you, you will be a regular Romeo,

a dashing Don Juan. Girls will swoon (whatever the heck that means) whenever you walk into the room. They will be lining up just to get your attention.

Okay . . . maybe not. Actually, probably not. But you *will* be a little less confused about how all this romantic girl-boy stuff is supposed to work. That much I can guarantee. So what are you waiting for? Let's get cracking!

>> What's Happening, Hot Stuff? <<

For starters, you are probably wondering why you suddenly care about girls at all. Not so long ago, sports, or your PlayStation, or your guitar, or books, or whatever it is you're into, was all you needed to be happy. Well, say good-bye to those simple days. Once you hit puberty, you start to become an adult, sexual being. For guys, this usually starts to happen between the ages of nine and twelve. Your body's changes are usually complete by the time you are in your late teens.

Chemicals in your body called hormones kick in and start to mix things up inside of you. They change you physically from a boy into a man. In other words, hormones—and the hormone testosterone in particular—trigger the changes in your body that turn you into adult. Hormones change your voice, making it deeper; trigger the growth of underarm, chest, facial, and pubic hair; and cause the growth of your penis and the onset of wet dreams and spontaneous erections.

You will probably learn all about these things in

school or from your parents. (You can also read *You Ought to Know: A Guy's Guide to Sex* for the full low-down on what your body goes through during puberty.) The newly active hormones in your body are also responsible for your changing feelings toward girls.

Maybe you've always had a crush on a girl you think is really pretty. Or maybe you've always thought all girls were really annoying. Either way, once puberty hits, you are probably going to start enjoying their company—or at least enjoy looking at them—more than you used to.

Maybe you are a romantic at heart. Or maybe you think all that love stuff isn't for you. Either way, there will probably be a girl who makes you feel kind of funny.

Maybe seeing her makes you feel nervous, or sick to your stomach, or clumsy, or silly, or speechless, or just plain stupid. Maybe you'll get an erection

Caution! Hormones at Work

when she simply passes you in the hallway. Either way, you are probably wondering if you are some kind of freak. My job is to assure you that you are definitely not a freak.

The Good News:

Girls go through lots of changes during puberty, too. Like you, they are starting to take more notice of the opposite sex. (That would be you.)

More Good News:

Like you, girls are confused about what exactly this new kind of sexual attraction means and how exactly to deal with it. Which, when you think about it, is . . .

Really, Really Good News:

You're all in it together!

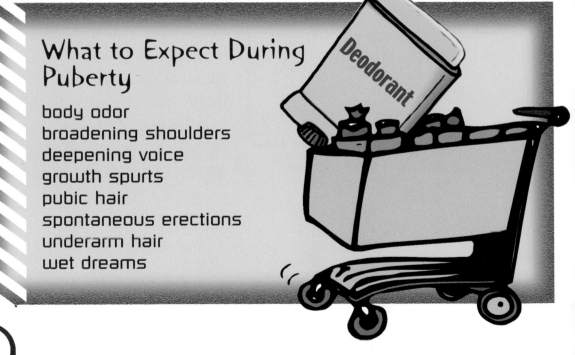

What to Expect During Puberty

body odor
broadening shoulders
deepening voice
growth spurts
pubic hair
spontaneous erections
underarm hair
wet dreams

>> But What If I'm Not "In It" at All? <<

If the guys around you are starting to show an interest in girls but you still aren't, don't stress out. It could be that you are developing at a slower rate. If you haven't seen any signs of puberty yet, be patient. Once those hormones really start working, you will feel the stirrings of romantic and physical interest in girls.

Also, you should know that your sexuality is just one aspect of your personality. Some people are more interested in having romantic and sexual relationships than others. This is true for people going through puberty and it's true for adults, too. Some people can't live without romance, love, and sex, while others can take it or leave it.

Maybe you are worried about big adult issues like pregnancy and sexually transmitted diseases like AIDS. Maybe you have decided that you really want to stay a kid for a while longer. Good for you. Do whatever feels right.

The Bottom Line:

If you don't have any interest in dating girls right now, don't worry about it! There's plenty of other stuff in life worth doing. But if you still want to know more, read on.

I Think I Might Be Gay

If after puberty you still find yourself more interested in the company of guys—maybe you have even developed really strong feelings for someone in particular—it could be that you are gay. People who are gay are romantically and sexually attracted to people of the same sex.

If you think that you are gay, there is no reason to stress out. Just see what happens naturally. Most guys go through a phase during puberty in which they find themselves attracted to other guys. Many eventually prefer women as sexual partners and romantic companions. But some don't, and that's okay, too. Puberty can be a confusing time, so try to be true to yourself, whoever you are.

Since most romantic relationships are initially based on friendship, we should talk a little about the "friends" thing first.

Once upon a time, not so long ago, it was rare for men and women to be close friends. Men and women didn't really hang out together. Basically, you lived with your parents until you met a girl, got married, and then started a family. You never even had much of a chance to develop relation- ships with women other than your wife.

Back in the day, most people married and had kids at a young age.

Today, thankfully, things are different. Many people get married much later in life, and some don't get married at all. Men and women now spend lots of fun years as single people, with both male and female friends. So you should consider yourself lucky. You were born during a period in time when people are more accepting of platonic (or non-sexual) relationships between guys and girls.

Why is that lucky? Because you can learn a lot about yourself by becoming friends with girls. You can also learn a lot about the kind of girl you want to be with romantically. Besides, girls know about other girls. So when you meet a girl you really like who makes you tongue-tied, it will come in real handy to have girl friends to whom you can actually turn to for advice.

The Bottom Line:
Hanging out with girls is different than hanging out with guys—even if you are just friends. You will find yourself talking about different kinds of things and in different ways. As a result, having both male and female friends makes life more interesting.

>>Yeah, But We Can't All Be Mulder And Scully<<

Fans of *The X-Files* know that FBI agents Fox Mulder and Dana Scully—great friends and partners—have never even really kissed. They have a cool relationship, but a Mulder and Scully thing is much harder to pull off in real life. After all, you can't believe everything you see on TV, right?

Katie and I have known each other for years. We used to do everything together. But something changed last summer and I'm not sure what to do about it. Like, if Katie knows that I like another girl, she starts saying stuff about her. Not awful stuff, but not nice stuff either. It makes me not want to talk to her the way I used to, and that makes me sad. Katie's really cool, but I don't like her like that. I just want my buddy back. —Tim, 14

13

It really annoys me that Cindy basically dropped me the second she got a boyfriend. They're not even going out anymore, but she says that if we start hanging out again the way we used to, people will think we're a couple. I just think she's way too into the idea of having a boyfriend. It's like her whole life revolves around getting whatever guy she likes this week. She's not going to have any friends left if she treats them all the way she treats me. And these guys she dates? Lo-hoo-hoo-sers! I don't understand why she won't date someone like me. Maybe even me!—Noah, 15

>> "Just" Friends <<

The problem with opposite-sex friendships is that sometimes (okay, a lot of times), either the guy or the girl wants the friendship to become something romantic. It can get kind of complicated. How do you deal if your female friend seems to want more than you want to give?

Well, as a general rule, if you don't like a girl romantically, never let her think that you do. For example, if you catch yourself flirting with a girl you don't really like (maybe to make someone else jealous), stop yourself.

If a girl whom you think of as just a friend brings up the subject of liking you, tell her that you really enjoy her friendship and hanging out with her, but that you don't have romantic feelings for her. She may be hurt, but she'll get over it. Being honest about it saves her more pain, and it will also spare you from feeling guilty about misleading her.

What's Flirting, Anyway?

Flirting is really hard to explain. It's like you only know what it is while you're doing it. Basically, it includes all sorts of behaviors that show another person that you are interested in them romantically. You may smile a lot. You may make eye contact, hold it, look away, and then look back. You may brush your arm against hers by "accident."

Flirting really has more to do with an attitude than with any specific action. If a girl touches your arm while she is talking to you, or flips her hair a lot, or asks you when your birthday is, or how tall you are, she is probably flirting.

>> But Maybe I Do Like Her . . . <<

Okay: You've got a best girl friend. Suddenly, you find yourself wanting to run your fingers through her hair, or take her out someplace nice, or kiss her, or call her just to hear her voice. Maybe you realize that you hate all of her boyfriends. This means that you like her, and that you may have a decision to make.

Do you tell her? Do you try to turn your friendship into something else? First, you need to decide whether or not you think she wants to be more than just friends. If you are pretty sure she does, then go for it, you stud!

But if you are unsure of how she feels, you need to decide what is more important to you—making your feelings known or keeping your friendship intact. If you tell her, and she doesn't like you "that way," she might get all weird on you. Is that a chance you are willing to take?

The Bottom Line:

Things will change once you let the cat out of the bag. If your friendship really matters to both of you, however, you can usually get it back on track.

Before you go professing your love to your gal pal, let's take a closer look at what exactly you may be getting yourself into.

3

<<< Dating, Kissing, Romance, and All That Girly Stuff >>>

Okay, so you're spending all your time thinking about her. You feel butterflies in your stomach whenever she's in the room. You write her love poems during study hall. You are completely into her.

Well, that's great. But I'll let you in on a little secret. She might be clueless that you like her. I mean, girls are great and all, but we're not psychic. So even if we think you like us, we want to know for sure. And that means that you have to tell us.

This, obviously, is the hard part. When you let someone else know that you like her, you open yourself up to rejection. The fact that she might laugh in your face and say, "You think that *I* would want to go out with *you?*" can put you in a cold sweat.

Okay, that probably won't happen. She might even like you back! But you'll never know if you don't ask. And if she is the kind of person that would laugh in your face (unless you're telling a really funny joke) you don't want to be with her anyway.

>> How Do I Get a Date? <<

The tough thing about dating for guys is that if you want a date, you are probably going to have to be the one to ask for it. Sometimes we girls do get up the courage to ask you out, but in general we like you to do it. Sorry! This may be changing, but replacing old-fashioned ways takes time.

If you aren't sure if a girl likes you and you want to find out, be sneaky about it—plan a group activity and include her. Then maybe you can get a chance to talk to her alone. See if it seems like she would want to do something with just you.

A date doesn't have to be a huge deal. You can ask her to do something casual on a Saturday afternoon if you are too nervous to try anything fancy. Ask her to do whatever you think she would most like to do. Then hold your breath and hope she says yes. If she doesn't, you're going to feel like an idiot, I guarantee it. We all get over rejection eventually, but be prepared for it just in case. Be ready to say, "Well, that's too bad" and make a quick exit. If you can say this and sound light-hearted, it sends the perfect message: No big deal, her loss!

Cool Date Ideas

1. Bowling. Healthy competition makes for great flirting possibilities.

2. A picnic. Ask your mom or someone who knows about these kinds of things to help you whip up some funky sandwiches, and then head to a nearby park.

3. A bike ride/run/in-line skating/hiking/ you get the idea. Having an activity to focus on makes you less nervous.

4. Go to a museum or a bookstore reading. Cultural dates give you stuff to talk about and show her that you are interested in the world around you.

5. Whatever she wants to do—even if it's going to see a "chick flick." There's nothing wrong with going with the flow if your girl wants to go to a candlemaking shop or a hockey game or a romantic movie. For whatever reason, girls tend to like tales of romance more than guys. Trust me, you'll live. And she'll like you all the more for being sensitive.

>> She Said Yes . . . Now What? <<

It's the oldest advice in the book. I can't believe I'm even going to say it, but I'm going to anyway. You know why? Because it's true! *Just be yourself.*

I could write out a dumb list to give you loads of ideas about how you should act on a date. But if something doesn't come naturally to you, it won't seem natural to your date, either.

If you are the outdoorsy type, go on an outdoorsy date—don't take her to a swanky restaurant. If you are a stylish guy, then take her to a teen club and show her those swing moves of yours. Don't suggest that you go hiking and then freak out because there are too many bugs.

Again, just be yourself. If you two go out again, it will be because she likes you because you're you, not because you behaved the way a guy "should" on a first date. This advice is also good for date number two through forever.

> More Advice to Last a Lifetime <

Be a gentleman. Do everything in your power to make sure that your date is having fun. Provide transportation if you can. Plan ahead. (In other words, check movie times, museum hours, etc., beforehand). Tell her that she looks nice (if she does) and that you had a nice time (if you did). Kiss her goodnight (if you want to). And expect her to treat you just as well as you treat her.

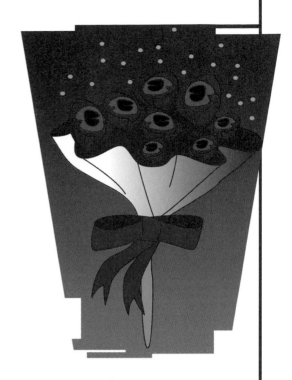

>> Never Been Kissed? <<

Everybody has a first kiss. And everybody gets nervous about it. If it hasn't happened to you yet, you probably wonder how or if it will ever happen at all. The good news is that you are probably more comfortable with the idea of kissing than the generations of kids who grew up before you. Maybe that's because there is a lot of kissing in the movies and on television these days. The most reassuring advice I can give is that you usually figure out how to kiss the moment you start doing it. (But here are a few pointers just in case.)

- Lean in and tilt your head (usually to the right). Let your lips softly caress hers.
- Follow her lead. If she is kissing you softly, it probably means that softly is how she likes to be kissed.
- Relax and enjoy it. Everyone has his or her own style of kissing. You don't have to do it a specific way for her to like it!

>> I Like Her, Alright, But My Life Ain't No *Dawson's Creek* <<

If you have ever watched *Dawson's Creek,* it may have made you feel as if there is something wrong with you if you haven't found your soulmate by the time you're sixteen. Dawson and Joey. Pacey and Andie. I mean, they're teenagers, but they act like they've already experienced the greatest love they'll ever know. Give me a break!

Sure, it happens occasionally. Someone falls in love with the girl or guy next door and that's it—end of story, happily ever after. But if the earth doesn't move when you are out with a girl, don't worry. Most people have to go on a *lot* of dates before they find someone they connect with in that incredible way. That shouldn't stop you from having plenty of fun relationships in the meantime.

The Bottom Line:
If you go out on a date and you have fun with that person, ask her out on another one. And then another. And then another. Before you know it, you might even have a girlfriend.

4

<<< Is She My "Girlfriend"? >>>

I love you

Having a girlfriend can be great. Being "in love" or even in "like" can add a little spring to your step no matter what. It's fun to have someone in your life whom you connect with, someone with whom you can share your inner-most thoughts—someone to day-dream about during a really boring school assembly. But if what you have actually qualifies as a real relation-ship—if you think of yourselves as a couple and other people do, too—things do change.

On top of that, if you and your girlfriend have a fight, you can't just walk away. If you hurt her feelings, you are going to have to deal with it. And if she hurts you, you are going to have to explain to her exactly why you are upset. Communication—the ability to name and share your feelings with someone else—is super-important.

>> Yeah, So What's Wrong with That? <<

Well, nothing. The fact that relationships are always changing is part of what makes them so great. So if you like a girl and want to spend time with her, you should—regardless of what anyone else says. But you may find that your friends will start acting weird once you have a girl-friend, especially if they don't. They might even make fun of you because you like spending time with a girl.

The Bottom Line:

Your friends are jealous. Or maybe they are confused about why you like girls when they don't (yet). Try to understand how your friends are feeling. Make sure that they know that no girl will ever take their place. After all, relationships come and go, but friends are forever, right?

You should also be careful not to spend all of your time with your girlfriend. A full life includes a lot of different kinds of relationships, with both girls and guys.

>> But I'm in LOVE! (I Think.) <<

Love is a really complicated thing. Sometimes you think you are in love with someone, and then you decide that you aren't. You may even decide that you never really loved her to begin with. And then you wonder why you thought you loved her if you really didn't, and whether you can avoid making the same mistake again.

These mind-boggling questions have been around forever. The answers are different for every person. For practical purposes, however, if you think you're in love, then you are. Your definition of love will probably change depending on what happens in your relationship. And it will change after the next relationship, and the next, and so on . . .

But try to keep these two things in mind along the way:

1. Being in love does not mean spending every waking moment with that person and controlling his or her life. A healthy and truly loving relationship allows both people the freedom to be individuals.
2. Being in love doesn't necessarily mean having sex. (Read on for more on that.)

Ten Things You Should Never Do to a Girl

1. Pressure her to do anything sexually.
2. Hit her.
3. Tell her that she's fat.
4. Tell her that she's stupid.
5. Cheat on her. (Have the courage to break up with her first.)
6. Say that you will die of pain if she doesn't have sex with you. (We know you won't.)
7. Call her names.
8. Lie to her.
9. Tell her that you love her when you don't.
10. Tell your friends about sexual things you've done with her—whether for real or in your imagination.

<<< Sex >>>

Sex, sex, sex. It's everywhere. You couldn't avoid it if you tried. Not that you would want to—sex can be great—but I'll let you in on a little secret. It ain't the be-all and end-all of existence.

Still, sooner or later, whether it is with your first girlfriend or your twentieth, you are going to think about having sex. And sooner or later, it will actually be a possibility and not just some fantasy. After you have been with a girl for a while, you might start touching her breasts while you're kissing, and the two of you might be curious to touch each other's genitals. This kind of touching can lead to sexual intercourse. Sexual intercourse is what most people mean when they say "having sex." It's when a man puts his penis inside a woman's vagina.

But there is really no hurry to have sex. In fact, there are a number of good reasons to wait. You may feel as if people around you are becoming more experienced than you, but that's okay. Everyone does things at his or her own pace. And a lot of times people aren't even doing the things that they say they are doing.

>> Why Wait? <<

People decide to wait to have sex for various reasons. Here are a few:

> AIDS and the HIV Virus <

HIV is the virus that causes the disease known as AIDS. Anyone can get AIDS—not just gay people, not just poor people, not just racial minorities. HIV is passed between people during sex through bodily fluids, like the semen that comes out of your penis or a woman's vaginal fluids. Just one sexual encounter with an infected person can expose you to the virus.

AIDS is a fatal disease that attacks the immune

The AIDS Quilt honors people who have died of AIDS.

system—the system that is supposed to protect your body from disease. Since a cure for AIDS has not yet been found, sex can be deadly if you sleep with an infected person. You can use a condom, but even condoms aren't a 100 percent guarantee against AIDS.

> Other Sexually Transmitted Diseases <

In addition to HIV, there are all sorts of diseases that you can catch from having sex. Some other sexually transmitted diseases include herpes, hepatitis, and chlamydia—and the list goes on. Some of them stay with you for life. Others are just plain unpleasant. And still others, like AIDS, are deadly.

> The Possibility of Pregnancy <

The act of sexual intercourse allows human reproduction to take place. If you don't use some kind of birth control (contraception), the girl you have sex with could become pregnant. Having a baby is a *huge* emotional and financial responsibility. It is a million times better to wait until you are an adult before bringing a child into the world.

> Emotional Reasons <

Sex is a very powerful experience. It can link you emotionally to the person that you have it with. People who have had sex at a young age often say later that they felt used or regretful. Once they are older, they realize that it was a mistake to have sex so young. They say that they chose the wrong person or that the experience wasn't as special as it should have been.

On the other hand, some people decide to wait to have sex until they are older. People who remain virgins until they go to college, for instance, often feel more in control of their sexual lives and more confident.

Needless to say, sex is a very personal decision. If you think that you should be in a big hurry to have sex because that is what everyone else is doing, think again. There are plenty of good reasons to wait—and plenty of people who do.

6

<<< Welcome to Dumpsville, Population: 1 >>>

One of the scariest things about love is that sometimes a person's feelings will suddenly change. And there is not really a whole lot that you can do about it. The trouble is, romantic feelings have a way of changing more quickly than other kinds of feelings. For example, if you love chocolate-chip ice cream today, odds are that you will love it tomorrow. But in relationships, things can change overnight.

>> What Are You Getting At? <<

Oh, alright already! All of this is just a roundabout way of saying that sooner or later, at least once, you will

probably get dumped. And odds are that you are not going to like it. You'll want to know *why*. You will want to know what you can do and how you can change to make things better. And then you will swear that you are never going to open up to anyone again.

You'll be miserable. You will feel crushed, mad, and confused. You might even be weepy. And while all of this may seem pointless—since you know that you can't change what somebody else feels in her heart—this mourning process is a natural part of any break-up. You have to let yourself feel what you're feeling.

You do not, however, need to wallow in it. Remember that living well is the best revenge. Not that it's revenge exactly that you are looking for. But there is something to be said for realizing that the girl who dumped you was a fool for doing so. So if you've been dumped, get busy living your life again. Fill up your calendar with stuff to do: Take up a new hobby, ask another girl out. In time—as hard as it is to believe, as much as you loved her, as beautiful as she is—you will be as good as new. And stronger for it.

>> What If I'm the One Who Wants Out? <<

Even if you are the one who is doing the breaking up, it's never easy to end a relationship. There is a natural tendency to blame the other person, or to view the whole relationship as a failure on one person's part. But we all get dumped sometimes, and we all dump other people. That's just the way it works.

Sometimes, you really like someone—until you get to know her better. Sometimes she isn't who you thought she was. And sometimes when someone really likes you a lot but you don't like her back, there is a tendency to think, "What's wrong with me that I don't like this person? She's smart and pretty and great."

It's one of the great mysteries of the world that no

matter how great a person seems, you might not feel anything for him or her in your heart. So stop beating yourself up and let the person go. Tell her you just don't think things are working out, and let her find someone else. Once she does, you might feel awful all over again. But if you broke up with her, you did it because it was the right thing for you to do. It's time to move on.

>> But Shouldn't I Try to Stick It Out? <<

Since most relationships have their ups and downs, it is best not to high-tail it out at your first fight. But there are a few situations where it is just best to get out. Here they are:

If your relationship has turned into a trauma-rama, it is probably time to call it quits. If you spend more time talking about your relationship and what is wrong with it than you do just having fun together, move on.

If your girlfriend is a green-eyed monster, it's time to adjust the color on your set. Jealousy is a natural emotion, but acting on it can be destructive. If your girl is telling you what to do, or who you can or can't see or talk to, tell her that you are your own person and that you will do whatever you please. If she won't let you live your own life, cut her loose.

If your girl makes you crazy or so mad you don't know what to do about it, get out before you hurt her or yourself. Relationships are supposed to bring happiness into our lives. If she is just making you crazy, break it off and spend some time alone to deal with your feelings.

If all you and your girl do is get physical every time you are together, it's probably a sign that you don't have a whole lot in common. While it's nice to be attracted to someone physically, it is better to find someone who excites your mind while sending flutters through your heart.

>>Breaking Up is Hard to Do . . . <<

There is nothing worse than hearing one of the old standard break-up lines. But the truth is that these feelings happen in many a split-up. Sometimes we really do blame ourselves, and we really do even want to stay friends.

So when a girl says, "It's not you, it's me," it means that she thinks you are great but that she can't figure out why she doesn't feel everything she should be feeling for you. It still hurts, sure. But at least it is proof that you aren't a jerk, and that other girls will like you, too. Wanting to stay friends basically means the same thing.

Of course, if a girl wants to stay friends with you after you have been a couple, you are probably going to have mixed feelings about it. You may want to say no to friend-ship, thinking that it will help to win her back. Because how could she possibly live without you, right?

Well, you can try this strategy, but I don't recommend it. You can totally cut her off and *really* show her, but it probably won't work. And then you will have lost a girl-friend and a friend, too.

The Bottom Line:

If a girl tells you that she just wants to be friends, she means it. Her reasons might not be clear to you—or even to her. However, trying to get her to change her mind and get back together with you is like banging your head against a wall. Save yourself the trouble and the pain. Take some time to let your feelings heal a little. Hang out with your old pals. Then see if you can be around her without feeling

angry, hurt, or jealous. Often, after a period of time, you will find that being friends with an ex-girlfriend isn't as hard as you thought it would be.

And, if you're lucky, you will realize that some of the ex-girlfriends that you decide to stay friends with will end up being some of the best friends you'll have. That's kind of a happy ending, right?

Top Five Reasons to Stay Friends

1. She's the only person in town with decent taste in music.
2. She knows all of your little flaws and still doesn't mind hanging out with you.
3. She's got cute friends.
4. She's got a swimming pool.

5. You still love her, but you aren't *in* love with her. There's a difference, ya know.

I know what you're thinking. You're thinking, "You can't be serious!" But let me explain.

Relationships aren't always easy. But like almost everything else in life, you will usually find that the good out- weighs the bad. In truth, there is a lot of exaggeration about how hard it is for men and women to get together and get along.

Girls are really not all that different from you. We all want to find someone that we like to be with—someone with whom we have things in common, and who also has other interests and can expose us to new things. We all want someone who will make us laugh and feel alive.

Maybe you have already met that person. Maybe you haven't. (You probably haven't.) But whatever your experience with romantic relationships, know this: Experience teaches you things that you need to learn about yourself.

It might not feel that way right now. You may feel as though getting the attention of a certain girl is the

only thing that matters in the world. But if you believe in any kind of cosmic sense of order in the universe (oh, just bear with me and keep reading), you will eventually see how you were meant to be with a certain someone at a certain time. Or maybe you will see that you were not meant to be with that person. And instead you needed to learn a lesson about life or yourself from the experience.

In the meantime, there is a lot of fun to be had with girls and dating and all that stuff. So what are you hanging around with me for?

Go on, get out of here! Scram!

<<< What's the Word? >>>

condom   A sleeve made of latex that slides over the penis to collect sperm when a man ejaculates. It helps to prevent pregnancy and the spread of sexually transmitted diseases.

contraception   Devices like condoms or birth control pills that are used to prevent pregnancy.

erection   When the penis is in an aroused, erect, or hardened state.

genitals   Sexual organs. For men, these are the penis and testicles; for women, the labia, clitoris, and vagina.

hormones   A product of living cells that circulate in the body and produce a specific effect on the body's appearance and its functions.

puberty   The period during which someone first becomes capable of reproducing sexually; marked by maturing of the genitals, development of secondary sex characteristics (like pubic hair), and menstruation (in females).

pubic hair   Hair that grows on or around the genitals, or sex parts, of a man or woman.

reproduction   The process by which a species creates new life. In the case of humans, this is through sexual intercourse.

semen   The white fluid released by the man, which contains sperm.

spontaneous erection   An erection that happens without sexual stimulation of any kind, frequent during puberty.

virgin   Someone who has never had sexual intercourse.

wet dreams   Also known as nocturnal emissions, when a man ejaculates, or releases semen, in his sleep.

Movies

Angus, 1995.
Say Anything, 1989.

Organizations

In the United States

Planned Parenthood Federation of America
810 Seventh Avenue
New York, NY 10019
(800) 829-7732
(212) 541-7800
Web site: http://www.plannedparenthood.org

Sexuality Information and Education Council of the United
   States (SIECUS)
130 West 42nd Street, Suite 350
New York, NY 10036
(212) 819-9770
Web site: http://www.siecus.orgSmart Date
P.O. Box 13232

San Luis Obispo, CA 93406
(805) 546-4941
e-mail: info@smartdate.com
Web site: http://www.smartdate.com

In Canada

Planned Parenthood Federation of Canada
1 Nicholas Street, Suite 430
Ottawa, Ontario K1N 7B7
(613) 241-4474
e-mail: admin@ppfc.ca
Web site: http://www.ppfc.ca/

Web Sites

KidsHealth.org
http://kidshealth.org

Planned Parenthood Federation of America's Teenwire
http://www.teenwire.com

VirtualKid
http://www.virtualkid.com

<<< By the Book >>>

Bell, Ruth. *Changing Bodies, Changing Lives: A Book for Teens on Sex and Relationships*. New York: Times, 1998.

Bourgeois, Paulette, et al. *Changes in You and Me: A Book about Puberty, Mostly for Boys*. New York: Perigee, 1994.

Glassman, Bruce S. *Everything You Need to Know About Growing Up Male*. New York: Rosen Publishing Group, 1995.

Madaras, Lynda. *My Body, My Self for Boys: The "What's Happening to My Body?" Workbook for Boys*. New York: Newmarket, 1995.

Many, Paul. *These Are the Rules*. New York: Walker, 1997.

McCoy, Kathy. *Life Happens: A Teenager's Guide to Friends, Failure, Sexuality, Love, Rejection, Addiction, Peer Pressure, Families, Loss, Depression, Change and Other Challenges of Living*. New York: Berkeley, 1996.

McCoy, Kathy, et al. *The New Teenage Body Book*. New York: Perigee, 1992.

Moe, Barbara. *Everything You Need to Know About Sexual Abstinence*. New York: Rosen Publishing Group, 1998.

Sommers, Michael. *Everything You Need to Know About Looking and Feeling Your Best: A Guide for Young Men*. New York: Rosen Publishing Group, 1999.

Zindel, Paul. *My Darling, My Hamburger*. New York: Bantam, 1984.

<<< Index >>>

<<< Credits >>>

About the Author
Tara E. Kelly is a freelance writer who lives in Brooklyn.

Photo Credits
Cover, pp. 5, 18, 19, 24, 30, 38 by Thaddeus Harden; pp. 9, 12, 19, 39 by Christine Walker; p. 11 © Arthur Tilley; pp. 16, 32 by Steve Skjold; pp. 20, 27, 33 by Scott Bauer; pp. 22, 26, 42 © Artville; p. 40 © Stephen Simpson.

Series Design and Layout
Oliver H. Rosenberg

Series Editor
Amy Haugesag